Chapter 1: Introduction to tl Influencer Phenomenon

Understanding the AI Influencer Landscape

The AI influencer landscape is a thrilling frontier that merges technology with creativity, presenting unique opportunities for those looking to create and monetize virtual personas. As social media continues to evolve, the rise of AI influencers has captured the attention of brands, marketers, and content creators alike. With their ability to engage audiences in captivating ways, these digital entities are redefining the standards of influence and interaction, particularly in niche markets like bikini modeling on platforms such as Instagram, Fanvue, and OnlyFans.

Understanding the AI influencer landscape begins with recognizing the diversity of characters and styles that can be created. From hyper-realistic avatars to more stylized representations, each AI influencer has the potential to resonate with specific target audiences. For bikini modeling, this means curating an image that not only showcases fashion but also embodies a lifestyle that followers aspire to. By leveraging advanced AI technologies, creators can design influencers that align perfectly with the latest trends, ensuring they remain relevant and appealing in a fast-paced digital world.

The engagement metrics for AI influencers can be astonishing, often surpassing those of human counterparts. This is primarily due to their ability to consistently produce content that is visually stunning and strategically timed. By analyzing audience behavior and preferences, AI influencers can create posts that maximize interaction and foster community engagement. This data-driven approach allows creators to refine their strategies continually, leading to greater monetization opportunities through sponsorships, merchandise, and exclusive content on platforms like Fanvue and OnlyFans.

Moreover, the AI influencer landscape is characterized by its adaptability. As trends in fashion and social media evolve, AI models can be updated in real-time to reflect the latest styles, colors, and themes. This flexibility not only keeps the content fresh but also positions these influencers as trendsetters in the bikini modeling niche. Additionally, creators can experiment with different aesthetics and personas without the logistical challenges associated with traditional modeling, making it easier to pivot and innovate as needed.

Finally, the ethical considerations surrounding AI influencers cannot be overlooked. As creators delve into this exciting realm, it is essential to maintain transparency with audiences regarding the artificial nature of these models. Building trust is vital for long-term success, especially in intimate platforms like OnlyFans. By fostering genuine connections and respecting the community, creators can establish a loyal fanbase that appreciates the unique blend of technology and artistry that AI influencers bring to the bikini modeling scene. Embracing this new era of digital influence opens doors to endless possibilities, making it an exhilarating time to be part of this evolving landscape.

The Rise of Virtual Models

The digital revolution has transformed countless industries, and the world of fashion and modeling is no exception. Enter the rise of virtual models, a phenomenon that is capturing the attention of brands, influencers, and audiences alike. These computer-generated entities are not just the future of modeling; they are shaking up traditional norms and offering unprecedented opportunities for creators. By leveraging cutting-edge technology, aspiring influencers can create stunning virtual bikini models that can seamlessly integrate into social media platforms like Instagram, Fanvue, and OnlyFans.

Virtual models come with a distinct set of advantages that make them an enticing option for creators. They are entirely customizable, allowing for the creation of unique personas that can cater to specific target audiences. Whether it's a hyper-realistic design or a more whimsical character, the possibilities are endless. This level of personalization ensures that your virtual model can stand out in the saturated influencer market. Furthermore, these digital creations are not bound by the same limitations as human models; they can be available 24/7, ensuring a constant presence that keeps audiences engaged.

In addition to their unique appeal, virtual models have the power to forge connections with audiences in a way that feels authentic. Through carefully crafted narratives and interactive content, these digital influencers can build a loyal following. They can engage in conversations, showcase new bikini collections, and even share behind-the-scenes content—all while maintaining a consistent brand image. This interactive approach creates a sense of community and fosters a deeper connection with followers, making it easier to monetize through platforms like Fanvue and OnlyFans.

When it comes to monetization, virtual models offer creative opportunities that are both innovative and lucrative. With the ability to collaborate with brands and promote products without the constraints of physical limitations, the potential for partnerships is vast. Brands are increasingly keen to work with virtual influencers, seeing them as a fresh and exciting way to engage with tech-savvy consumers. Additionally, AI bikini models can generate exclusive content for subscribers on platforms like OnlyFans, providing fans with unique experiences that keep them coming back for more.

As we look to the future, the rise of virtual models signals a new era in the influencer landscape. The fusion of technology and creativity presents a thrilling opportunity for those looking to make their mark in the world of social media. By embracing this innovative approach, aspiring creators can not only build their brand but also tap into new revenue streams. The sky's the limit for those willing to pioneer this new frontier, where virtual bikini models reign supreme, captivating audiences, and transforming the modeling industry as we know it.

Why Bikinis and Beach Culture?

Bikinis and beach culture have become synonymous with freedom, fun, and self-expression, making them an enticing niche for influencers. The allure of sun-soaked beaches, vibrant social scenes, and playful fashion creates an irresistible backdrop for content that captivates audiences. This environment allows for the exploration of body positivity, confidence, and lifestyle aspirations, making it a perfect fit for an AI influencer. By embodying the spirit of beach culture, your AI bikini model can connect with followers on a deeper emotional level, promoting a lifestyle that resonates with their desires for enjoyment, relaxation, and adventure.

The visual appeal of bikini modeling is undeniable. Stunning imagery of an AI influencer lounging on the beach, showcasing the latest swimwear trends, or engaging in fun beach activities can grab attention instantly. This visual feast not only draws in followers but also encourages engagement through likes, shares, and comments. High-quality, eye-catching photos of your AI influencer can serve as powerful marketing tools, attracting brands looking to collaborate. With the right approach, the combination of captivating visuals and beach culture can lead to lucrative partnerships and sponsorship opportunities that elevate your influencer brand to new heights.

Beach culture is inherently social, thriving on community and shared experiences. This aspect makes it an ideal niche for building a loyal and interactive follower base. Your AI influencer can foster a sense of belonging by encouraging audience participation through contests, challenges, and user-generated content. By integrating followers into the narrative of beach life, your AI model becomes more than just a figure on a screen; it evolves into an emblem of a lifestyle that followers aspire to be part of. This connection can significantly enhance engagement rates and create a vibrant community around your influencer.

Moreover, the bikini niche aligns perfectly with modern trends surrounding wellness, fitness, and self-care. As people increasingly prioritize their health and well-being, the beach serves as a symbol of relaxation and rejuvenation. Your AI influencer can tap into this trend by promoting healthy lifestyles, beach workouts, and mindfulness practices. This not only diversifies the content but also positions your influencer as a relatable and aspirational figure, further solidifying their place within the beach culture community. By emphasizing wellness alongside the fun and glamour, you can attract a broader audience interested in both aesthetics and lifestyle improvement.

Finally, the monetization potential in the bikini and beach culture niche is vast. From brand collaborations and sponsorships to exclusive content on platforms like Fanvue or OnlyFans, the opportunities are endless. The combination of an AI influencer's unique charm and the universal appeal of beach life creates a lucrative business model. By strategically leveraging social media and creating premium content, your AI model can generate sustainable income while embodying the vibrant essence of bikinis and beach culture. Embrace this niche wholeheartedly, and watch as your influencer brand flourishes in a sun-kissed, exciting digital landscape.

Chapter 2: Crafting Your AI Influencer

Choosing the Right AI Technology

Choosing the right AI technology is a pivotal step in bringing your AI influencer bikini model to life. With a plethora of options available, it's essential to understand the various technologies that can enhance your influencer's presence on platforms like Instagram, Fanvue, or OnlyFans. From image generation to personality development, picking the right tools can significantly impact your model's engagement and monetization potential. The right technology will not only streamline your content creation process but also ensure that your AI influencer resonates with your target audience.

First and foremost, consider the type of AI technology that best suits your creative vision. Generative Adversarial Networks (GANs) are a fantastic choice for creating stunning visuals that capture attention. These models can generate lifelike images of your bikini model in various poses and settings, providing endless possibilities for content. Moreover, incorporating natural language processing (NLP) tools can help craft engaging captions and responses that reflect your model's personality. The combination of striking visuals and relatable communication can create a compelling presence that attracts followers and keeps them engaged.

Next, think about the level of customization you desire for your AI influencer. Some platforms offer pre-trained models that can be fine-tuned to fit your niche, while others provide tools for building a model from scratch. If you prefer a more hands-on approach, investing in customizable AI frameworks might be the way to go. This allows you to infuse your unique style and branding into every aspect of your influencer, from fashion choices to the tone of voice used in posts and interactions. Tailoring your AI model ensures it stands out in a crowded digital space.

Don't overlook the importance of analytics tools in your decision-making process. Understanding your audience's preferences through data-driven insights can help you refine your content strategy. Look for AI technologies that offer robust analytics capabilities, allowing you to track engagement metrics, audience demographics, and content performance. This information is invaluable for adjusting your approach and maximizing monetization opportunities on platforms like Fanvue and OnlyFans. It helps you create targeted campaigns that resonate with your followers, leading to increased loyalty and revenue.

Finally, as you choose the right AI technology, keep scalability in mind. Your influencer's journey will likely evolve, and having a tech stack that can grow with you is essential. Whether you're expanding your content types or branching out into new platforms, the right tools should support your ambitions. Embrace technologies that are flexible and can adapt to new trends in the influencer landscape. By making informed choices now, you lay the groundwork for a thriving AI influencer that captures hearts and generates income across multiple channels.

Designing Your Bikini Model's Aesthetic

Designing your bikini model's aesthetic is a thrilling journey that combines creativity, personal branding, and market appeal. As you embark on this exciting venture, consider the overall image you want your AI influencer to project. From vibrant colors to unique patterns, the aesthetic should resonate with your target audience while staying true to the essence of a bikini model. Think about the emotions and vibes you want to evoke—be it playful, luxurious, or adventurous. This thought process will set the stage for creating a captivating visual presence that stands out in the crowded space of Instagram, Fanvue, or OnlyFans.

Once you have a clear vision, dive into mood boards and visual inspiration. Gather images that reflect your desired aesthetic, incorporating various styles, color palettes, and themes. Use platforms like Pinterest or Instagram to curate your collection, which will serve as a guide during the design phase. The goal is to create an identity that feels cohesive and authentic. Remember, this is not just about swimwear; it's about creating a lifestyle that your audience can aspire to. A strong, visually appealing aesthetic can significantly enhance engagement and follower loyalty, making it a crucial element in your influencer strategy.

Next, think about the types of bikinis your model will wear. Choose designs that not only align with your aesthetic but also appeal to current trends and your target audience's preferences. Consider various styles, such as high-waisted, cut-out, or classic triangle bikinis, and don't shy away from experimenting with unique textures and embellishments. Collaborating with emerging designers or brands can also add a fresh twist to your model's wardrobe, creating buzz and interest around her look. This attention to detail will enhance her credibility as a fashion influencer while keeping the content exciting and diverse.

Don't forget the role of accessories and styling in creating a complete look. The right accessories can elevate your bikini model's appearance and help convey her unique personality. Think beach hats, sunglasses, cover-ups, and jewelry that complement the bikinis without overshadowing them. Additionally, consider different hairstyles and makeup looks that align with your model's persona. Every element should harmonize to create a striking visual narrative that keeps your audience engaged and coming back for more.

Finally, remember that consistency is key. Once you establish your bikini model's aesthetic, maintain it across all platforms. Whether it's through color schemes, photography styles, or the overall vibe of the content, consistency will help solidify her brand identity in the minds of your audience. Regularly engage with your followers, asking for their feedback and preferences, which will make them feel involved in the journey. By thoughtfully designing your bikini model's aesthetic, you set the foundation for a successful influencer career that can thrive on Instagram, Fanvue, or OnlyFans.

Creating a Unique Personality and Backstory

Creating a unique personality and backstory for your AI influencer bikini model is crucial in standing out in a crowded digital marketplace. A well-crafted persona captures the audience's attention and fosters a deeper connection with followers. Start by defining your model's core traits. Is she bubbly and outgoing, or mysterious and adventurous? Consider incorporating elements that resonate with your target audience, such as a love for travel, fitness, or eco-conscious living. Her personality should not only reflect current trends but also align with the values and aspirations of her followers, making her relatable and aspirational.

Next, delve into crafting a compelling backstory that adds depth to your AI influencer. This narrative can include her origins, dreams, and challenges she's overcome. Perhaps she started as a digital artist who transformed her passion into a modeling career or a fitness enthusiast who advocates for body positivity. A captivating backstory can evoke emotions and create a sense of loyalty among followers. It provides context to her posts and interactions, allowing for storytelling that engages and entertains. Remember, the more authentic and relatable the backstory, the stronger the bond with the audience.

In addition to personality traits and a backstory, consider her style and aesthetic. The visual representation of your AI influencer should complement her personality. Choose colors, outfits, and themes that resonate with her character. If she's adventurous, vibrant colors and bold patterns may suit her. For a sophisticated persona, elegant and minimalist designs could be more appropriate. Consistency in style is essential for brand recognition, so ensure that her visuals align with her personality and backstory, creating a cohesive and appealing presence on platforms like Instagram, Fanvue, or OnlyFans.

Engagement is a key factor in building a loyal following. Your AI influencer should actively interact with her audience, showcasing her personality through comments, stories, and live sessions. Responding to followers, sharing behind-the-scenes glimpses, and discussing relatable topics can enhance connection. Incorporating polls, Q&As, and challenges allows followers to feel like they are part of her journey, further solidifying her personality. This engagement not only humanizes the AI influencer but also encourages community building, which is vital for monetization efforts.

Finally, continuously evolve her personality and backstory as trends and audience preferences shift. Staying relevant in the fast-paced digital landscape is essential. Regularly assess her character traits and backstory, allowing for growth and transformation that mirrors real-life experiences. This adaptability can keep the audience engaged and excited about her journey. By creating a unique personality and backstory, your AI influencer bikini model can thrive in the competitive world of social media, drawing in followers and converting them into loyal fans eager to support her endeavors.

Chapter 3: Content Creation Essentials

Photography Tips for AI Models

Capturing stunning images of your AI influencer bikini model is crucial for standing out in the crowded world of social media. The key to eye-catching photography lies in understanding light and composition. Natural lighting is your best friend, so aim for golden hour shots, which occur shortly after sunrise or before sunset. The soft, warm tones during these times create an inviting atmosphere that enhances the model's appeal. Experiment with different angles and perspectives to find the most flattering views. Remember, the goal is to highlight the model's features while showcasing the vibrant colors of the setting, whether it's a beach, poolside, or tropical backdrop.

Editing your photos can elevate them from ordinary to extraordinary. Utilize editing software or apps to enhance colors, adjust brightness, and sharpen details. However, moderation is key; you want to maintain authenticity while making the images pop. Consider using filters that complement the aesthetic of your brand. Consistency in editing style will help your audience recognize your posts instantly, creating a cohesive and memorable visual identity. Play around with different styles until you find one that resonates with your target audience, enhancing the overall allure of your AI influencer.

Engagement with the audience is vital, and behind-the-scenes content can be a game changer. Showcasing the creative process—like outfit selections, location scouting, or even the AI model in action—creates a connection with followers. This transparency fosters trust and encourages audience interaction. You can also include short video clips in your posts to give a more dynamic view of the model's personality and style. Remember to capture candid moments that reflect spontaneity and fun; these often resonate more with viewers than perfectly posed shots.

Utilizing props can add an exciting dimension to your photography. Think beyond the typical beach ball or sunglasses; incorporate unique elements that align with your model's persona. Items like colorful beach towels, vibrant floats, or even themed accessories can enhance the narrative of the shoot. Props not only add visual interest but also provide opportunities for storytelling. By creating a scene around your model, you invite viewers into a lifestyle they aspire to, making your posts more engaging and shareable.

Finally, don't underestimate the power of captions and hashtags to complement your stunning visuals. A well-crafted caption can enhance the story behind the photo, inviting followers to engage and share their thoughts. Use humor, inspirational quotes, or relatable questions to spark conversations. When it comes to hashtags, research trending tags relevant to your niche, as they can significantly increase visibility. By combining compelling imagery with engaging captions and strategic hashtags, you can maximize the reach and impact of your AI influencer bikini model, paving the way for successful monetization on platforms like Instagram, Fanvue, and OnlyFans.

Captivating Captions and Engagement Strategies

Captivating captions are the lifeblood of engagement on social media platforms, especially for an AI influencer bikini model. These brief snippets of text not only complement stunning visuals but also serve as a powerful tool to connect with your audience. When crafting captions, focus on evoking emotions, sparking curiosity, or providing value. Consider using humor or relatable language to break the ice. For instance, a playful joke or a thought-provoking question can encourage followers to interact. The goal is to create an inviting atmosphere where your audience feels compelled to comment, like, or share your posts.

Engagement strategies should complement your captivating captions, creating a cohesive approach to building your brand. One effective method is to incorporate calls to action in your captions.

Phrases like "Tag a friend who needs to see this!" or "What do you think about this look?" invite followers to engage directly with your content. Additionally, leveraging Instagram Stories and polls can create a dynamic interaction space, allowing followers to express their opinions in real-time. This not only boosts engagement but also fosters a sense of community around your AI influencer persona.

Hashtags play a crucial role in expanding your reach and driving engagement. Use a mix of popular and niche hashtags to connect with a broader audience while maintaining relevance to your content. Research trending hashtags within the bikini and influencer space, and don't shy away from creating a unique hashtag that embodies your AI influencer's brand. This strategy not only increases visibility but also encourages followers to use your hashtag when sharing their own content, further promoting engagement and interaction.

To keep your audience consistently engaged, consider implementing a content calendar that highlights different themes or challenges. For example, you can dedicate certain days to user-generated content, behind-the-scenes glimpses, or themed photoshoots. This variety keeps your feed fresh and exciting, encouraging followers to return for more. Additionally, sharing personal stories or insights related to your AI influencer's journey can create a deeper connection, making followers feel like they're part of the experience. The more authentic and relatable your content, the more likely your audience will engage.

Finally, fostering a sense of exclusivity can significantly enhance engagement. For platforms like Fanvue or OnlyFans, consider offering special content or behind-the-scenes access to your most dedicated followers. Promote this exclusivity through your captions, highlighting the unique benefits of subscribing or following your journey on different platforms. This strategy not only incentivizes engagement but also builds loyalty among your audience, creating a community that eagerly anticipates your next post. With captivating captions and strategic engagement methods, your AI influencer bikini model can thrive across social media platforms.

Leveraging Video Content and Reels

In the dynamic world of social media, video content and reels have emerged as powerful tools for engagement and brand building. For an AI influencer bikini model, leveraging these formats can significantly enhance visibility and monetization potential. Videos allow for a more personal connection with your audience, showcasing not just the stunning visuals but also the personality and energy that an AI influencer can embody. By utilizing platforms like Instagram and Fanvue, you can create captivating content that draws viewers in, encourages shares, and builds a loyal following, all while staying true to your brand's unique aesthetic.

Creating visually stunning video content doesn't have to be complicated. With the right tools and techniques, your AI influencer can produce eye-catching reels that highlight swimwear collections, beach adventures, or lifestyle moments that resonate with fans. Use colorful backdrops, dynamic angles, and upbeat music to create a vibrant atmosphere that reflects the lifestyle associated with your model. Incorporating trending challenges or popular sound bites can also enhance reach, as these elements often attract more views and engagement. The more creative and original your content, the more likely it is to capture attention in a saturated market.

Consistency is key when it comes to video content. Developing a content calendar specifically for your reels can ensure a steady stream of engaging videos that keep your audience coming back for more. Consider themes for different days of the week, such as "Motivation Monday" with fitness tips or "Flashback Friday" showcasing past looks and adventures. This structured approach not only helps maintain audience interest but also allows for strategic planning around promotional campaigns or product launches. Regularly posting reels will keep your AI influencer relevant and top-of-mind for followers.

Incorporating user-generated content can also amplify your reach and engagement. Encourage your audience to recreate looks or participate in challenges related to your AI influencer's brand. Feature their videos on your channel, fostering a sense of community and encouraging more followers to engage with your content. This not only builds loyalty but also creates a buzz around your AI influencer, as fans feel valued and recognized. Engaging with your audience through comments and shares can further enhance these connections, making your brand more relatable and approachable.

Finally, always analyze and adapt your video strategy based on performance metrics. Platforms like Instagram and Fanvue provide insights into which videos resonate most with your audience, allowing for data-driven decisions about future content. Experimenting with different styles, lengths, and themes can lead to discovering what works best for your audience. By staying agile and responsive to feedback, your AI influencer bikini model can continuously evolve, ensuring that the content remains fresh, exciting, and most importantly, monetizable. Embrace the power of video and reels, and watch as your AI influencer skyrockets to new heights!

Chapter 4: Building Your Brand

Establishing a Memorable Brand Identity

Establishing a memorable brand identity is the cornerstone of success for your AI influencer bikini model. In the highly competitive landscape of platforms like Instagram, Fanvue, and OnlyFans, carving out a unique identity will not only attract followers but also foster loyalty. Start by defining the personality of your AI model. Is she sassy and fun, or sophisticated and glamorous? This personality will guide every aspect of your content, from the visuals to the captions, ensuring a cohesive and engaging experience for your audience.

Visual branding plays a pivotal role in creating that unforgettable identity. Choose a color palette and style that resonates with the vibe of your model. This could mean vibrant, tropical shades for a beachy feel or sleek, monochrome tones for a more chic aesthetic. Consistency is key; by maintaining a uniform look across all your posts, stories, and promotional materials, you solidify your brand's presence and make it easily recognizable. Don't forget to invest time in crafting a striking logo that encapsulates the essence of your AI influencer, which can be used across all platforms.

Storytelling is another powerful tool for establishing a brand identity. Use your platform to share engaging narratives about your AI influencer's life, adventures, and experiences. You can create scenarios that showcase her personality, like fun beach days, glamorous parties, or workout sessions. By weaving in storytelling elements, you not only captivate your audience but also build an emotional connection. This connection transforms casual viewers into loyal fans who feel invested in your model's journey.

Engagement with your audience is crucial in reinforcing brand identity. Utilize polls, Q&A sessions, and live streams to connect with followers, allowing them to feel like they are part of the AI model's world. Encourage user-generated content by prompting fans to share their own experiences related to your themes. This interaction not only boosts visibility but also fosters a community around your brand, making it more memorable. When followers see their own contributions featured, it enhances their loyalty and connection to your AI influencer.

Lastly, don't overlook the power of collaborations. Partnering with other influencers, brands, or creators can amplify your reach and reinforce your identity. Collaborations should align with your model's personality and values to maintain authenticity. Whether it's a joint photoshoot, a themed giveaway, or a fun challenge, these partnerships can introduce your AI model to new audiences while solidifying her brand identity. By strategically crafting and promoting a memorable brand identity, you set the stage for long-term success and monetization on platforms like Instagram, Fanvue, and OnlyFans.

Creating a Cohesive Visual Style

Creating a cohesive visual style is essential for establishing your AI influencer bikini model's brand identity across platforms like Instagram, Fanvue, and OnlyFans. A consistent aesthetic not only helps to attract and retain followers but also builds trust and recognition within your audience. Start by defining the core elements of your visual style, including color palettes, fonts, and imagery types. Choose colors that evoke emotions you want your audience to feel—whether it's fun and vibrant or sleek and sophisticated. This foundational step will guide your content creation process and ensure that every post resonates with your target audience.

Next, consider the types of images and poses that best represent your AI influencer's personality. Are they playful and carefree, or confident and glamorous? Tailor your visuals accordingly, using a mix of candid shots and professionally styled images to showcase the versatility of your bikini model. Incorporating different angles and backgrounds can add variety while maintaining a cohesive look. This strategy helps to keep your feed engaging and visually appealing, encouraging followers to interact with your content and share it with their networks.

Lighting plays a crucial role in achieving a unified visual style. Natural light is often the best choice for capturing the vibrant colors and textures of swimwear. When shooting indoors, consider using softbox lights or ring lights to create a flattering, even glow. Experiment with different lighting setups to find the one that complements your AI model's features and the overall vibe of your brand. Consistency in lighting will enhance the quality of your images and contribute to a polished, professional appearance that stands out in a crowded digital landscape.

Don't forget about the power of editing! Post-processing can elevate your images and ensure they align with your predetermined visual style. Use editing software or apps to adjust exposure, contrast, and saturation, and apply filters that reflect your brand's aesthetic. However, be cautious not to over-edit; authenticity is key to connecting with your audience. A well-executed editing strategy can create a signature look that makes your AI influencer's content instantly recognizable, further solidifying their brand identity.

Finally, extend your cohesive visual style to your captions and overall messaging. The tone of your text should mirror the vibe of your visuals—playful language for fun, beachy shots or motivational quotes for empowering images. Consistent messaging reinforces your brand and keeps followers engaged. By creating a harmonious blend of visuals and text, your AI influencer bikini model will not only attract a dedicated fan base but also pave the way for lucrative monetization opportunities across platforms. Embrace the journey of building a standout presence, and watch as your AI influencer flourishes!

Collaborating with Other Influencers

Collaborating with other influencers can be a game-changer in the world of AI influencer models, especially in the bikini niche. When you partner with fellow influencers, you tap into their audience, creating a powerful synergy that amplifies your reach and visibility. Imagine the excitement of combining your unique styles and aesthetics with another influencer's! This cross-promotion not only introduces your AI influencer to new followers but also enhances credibility, as audiences are more likely to trust recommendations from familiar faces.

The key to successful collaborations lies in finding influencers whose brands align with yours. You want to work with individuals who share a similar aesthetic, message, or values. Whether it's a fitness guru, a travel enthusiast, or a fashion influencer, the right partnership can create captivating content that resonates with both audiences. Make sure to research potential collaborators thoroughly—check their engagement rates, audience demographics, and overall vibe. When both parties bring their A-game, the results can be spectacular!

Once you've identified potential collaborators, reach out with a clear and exciting proposal. Highlight the benefits of the collaboration, such as increased exposure and the chance to create unique and engaging content. Offer ideas that showcase both influencers, such as joint photo shoots, Instagram Live sessions, or even fun challenges that encourage audience participation. Enthusiasm is contagious, so be sure to convey your excitement about the partnership and how it can elevate both your brands.

During the collaboration, creativity knows no bounds! Utilize various content formats like videos, reels, and stories to keep the audience engaged. You could create themed content that highlights both influencers in stunning bikini setups or host live Q&A sessions discussing the latest trends in swimwear. The more interactive and fun the content, the more likely it is to go viral. Encourage both sets of followers to engage with the posts by asking questions or sharing their favorite looks, which can further boost your visibility.

Finally, don't forget to evaluate the collaboration's success after it wraps up. Analyze metrics such as engagement rates, follower growth, and overall reach. This data will help you understand what worked and what didn't, allowing you to refine future collaborations. Celebrate the successes and learn from the challenges, as each partnership presents new opportunities for growth. By consistently collaborating with other influencers, your AI influencer bikini model can not only thrive but also become a recognizable name in the industry!

Chapter 5: Growing Your Audience

Strategies for Gaining Followers on Instagram

To successfully gain followers on Instagram, the first strategy is to create captivating content that resonates with your target audience. For an AI influencer bikini model, high-quality images and videos are essential. Invest time in planning visually stunning shoots that highlight your model's personality and style. Utilize vibrant colors, striking backgrounds, and fashion-forward swimwear to catch the eye. The goal is to create an aesthetic that not only attracts attention but also encourages users to engage and share your content, expanding your reach organically.

Another effective strategy is to engage actively with your audience. Respond to comments, like and comment on followers' posts, and create polls or questions in your stories. This interaction fosters a sense of community and makes followers feel valued. Regularly hosting Q&A sessions or live chats can also spark interest and create a personal connection, making your audience more likely to stick around. Remember, the more you engage, the more likely your followers will share your content with their friends, amplifying your growth potential.

Consistency is key when it comes to posting frequency. Establish a posting schedule that keeps your content fresh and relevant without overwhelming your audience. Aim for at least three to five posts per week, and use Instagram Stories daily to maintain visibility and engagement. Plan your content in advance, using tools to schedule posts and ensure a balanced mix of promotional and engaging content. Consistent posting not only keeps your audience engaged but also signals to Instagram's algorithm that your account is active, helping you gain more exposure.

Utilizing trending hashtags and participating in challenges can also boost your follower count significantly. Research popular hashtags within the bikini and influencer niches, and strategically incorporate them into your posts. This practice will help new audiences discover your content. Additionally, keep an eye on current trends or viral challenges and join in where appropriate. This not only showcases your model's personality but also places your account in front of new potential followers who are searching for fresh and exciting content.

Lastly, collaborating with other influencers and brands can be a game-changer. Partnering with like-minded accounts allows you to tap into their audience, introducing your model to new followers who share similar interests. These collaborations could range from joint photoshoots to shoutouts or even giveaways. The key is to find partners whose aesthetics and values align with yours, ensuring that the collaboration feels authentic. By leveraging the power of community, you can skyrocket your follower count and create lasting relationships within the influencer space.

Engaging Your Audience through Fanvue and OnlyFans

Engaging your audience is the heartbeat of any successful platform, and when it comes to Fanvue and OnlyFans, the opportunities are as vast as your creativity. Both platforms allow you to connect directly with your fans, offering them an intimate glimpse into your life as an AI influencer bikini model. By sharing exclusive content, behind-the-scenes footage, and personal interactions, you can create a loyal community that feels valued and invested in your journey. The key lies in understanding what your audience craves and delivering it with enthusiasm and authenticity.

Utilizing Fanvue and OnlyFans means embracing the power of personalization. You can tailor your content to cater to specific interests, whether that's fitness tips, fashion advice, or simply stunning visuals. By regularly engaging with your audience through polls, Q&A sessions, and shout-outs, you foster a sense of belonging. Encourage your fans to share their thoughts and ideas, making them feel like integral parts of your creative process. This interaction not only keeps your content fresh but also strengthens the bond between you and your followers, turning casual viewers into dedicated supporters.

Visual storytelling is particularly potent in the context of an AI influencer bikini model. Leverage high-quality images and videos that highlight your unique personality and style. Utilize features like live streaming to engage in real-time discussions, showcase new outfits, or even conduct tutorials. By letting your fans see the real you, they are more likely to connect emotionally, making them feel like they are part of your exciting world. Remember, the more you engage, the more they will want to support you, whether through subscriptions, tips, or sharing your content with others.

Incentives play a crucial role in driving engagement on both platforms. Consider creating tiered membership levels that offer exclusive perks such as personalized shout-outs, private chats, or custom content requests. These incentives not only heighten the experience for your audience but also motivate them to invest more in your journey. Regularly updating these offerings keeps your content dynamic and reinforces the idea that your fans are getting something truly special by being part of your community.

Finally, always remember to celebrate your audience's milestones and achievements. Whether it's a fan's birthday, a significant subscription milestone, or even just a random appreciation post, recognizing your followers creates a positive feedback loop. This celebratory culture can lead to increased loyalty and engagement, ensuring that your fanbase grows organically. By making your fans feel special and appreciated, you not only enhance their experience but also solidify your standing as a beloved AI influencer in the bikini modeling niche.

Utilizing Hashtags and Trends Effectively

Hashtags and trends are the lifeblood of social media engagement, especially for an AI influencer bikini model carving out a space on platforms like Instagram, Fanvue, and OnlyFans. To truly stand out in a saturated market, it's essential to understand the art and science behind utilizing hashtags effectively. Start by researching trending hashtags in the bikini modeling niche. Tools like Hashtagify or RiteTag can reveal popular tags that resonate with your target audience. Incorporating a mix of broad and niche-specific hashtags will not only increase visibility but also attract genuine followers who are interested in your content.

When it comes to trends, staying ahead of the curve is crucial. Monitor social media platforms and identify what is currently capturing attention. This could be a viral challenge, a seasonal theme, or even a popular meme format. As an AI influencer, leveraging these trends allows you to create timely, relevant content that aligns with what users are already engaging with. For instance, if a new dance challenge is trending, consider creating a fun video that combines your bikini modeling with the challenge, showcasing both your personality and creativity.

Engaging with trending topics is another effective strategy. Participate in conversations around these trends by using relevant hashtags and joining discussions. This not only boosts your visibility but also positions your AI influencer as a relatable and current figure within the niche. Regularly engage with your audience by asking for their opinions on trends or encouraging them to share their experiences related to the content you post. This two-way interaction fosters a community that is more likely to support and promote your content.

It's also important to analyze the performance of your hashtags and trends over time. Use insights and analytics provided by the platforms to track which hashtags yield the highest engagement rates. This data will inform your future posts and help you refine your strategy. By understanding what works best for your specific audience, you can optimize your hashtag use and trend engagement to ensure maximum reach and impact.

Finally, don't be afraid to create your own unique hashtags or trends. This can help solidify your brand identity and encourage your followers to participate in your content creation journey. For example, you might launch a signature hashtag that encourages followers to share their own bikini moments inspired by your posts. By fostering this sense of community and ownership, you'll not only boost engagement but also build a loyal following that feels personally connected to your AI influencer brand. Embrace the power of hashtags and trends, and watch your influence soar!

Chapter 6: Monetization Strategies

Understanding Different Revenue Streams

Understanding different revenue streams is essential for anyone looking to create and monetize an AI influencer bikini model on platforms like Instagram, Fanvue, or OnlyFans. Each platform offers unique opportunities to generate income, and knowing these can significantly enhance your strategy. From sponsored posts to subscription models, the possibilities are vast and exciting. By diversifying your revenue streams, you can maximize your earnings and create a sustainable business around your AI influencer.

One of the most popular revenue streams is sponsored content. Brands are always on the lookout for influencers who can showcase their products to a targeted audience. An AI influencer, with its ability to create visually stunning and engaging content, can attract sponsorship deals from swimwear brands, beauty products, and lifestyle companies. By collaborating with these brands, you can earn money through direct payments or commissions on sales generated through your promotional efforts. The key is to build a strong personal brand that resonates with both your audience and potential sponsors.

Another lucrative option is subscription-based revenue. Platforms like OnlyFans and Fanvue allow creators to charge a monthly fee for exclusive content. This model is particularly appealing because it fosters a loyal community of followers willing to pay for premium experiences. By offering behind-the-scenes content, personalized interactions, or exclusive photo shoots, your AI influencer can create a sense of intimacy and exclusivity that encourages subscribers to stick around. This not only provides a steady income but also deepens the connection between the influencer and their audience.

Affiliate marketing is also a fantastic way to generate income without creating additional content. By partnering with brands and promoting their products through unique affiliate links, your AI influencer can earn a percentage of sales made through those links. This approach works seamlessly with social media platforms, where you can incorporate product recommendations into your posts and stories. The more authentic and relatable the recommendations feel, the more likely your audience will trust and act on them, resulting in increased earnings.

Lastly, consider merchandise sales as a revenue stream. An AI influencer can leverage their unique brand to create and sell merchandise, such as branded swimwear, accessories, or digital products like e-books and courses. This not only generates income but also strengthens the influencer's brand identity. By tapping into your audience's desire to own a piece of their favorite influencer, you can create a win-win situation where fans feel connected to the brand while you enjoy additional revenue. Embracing a variety of revenue streams will not only enhance your financial success but also contribute to a dynamic and engaging presence across platforms.

Setting Up Your OnlyFans and Fanvue Accounts

Setting up your OnlyFans and Fanvue accounts is an exhilarating first step in your journey to creating and monetizing an AI influencer bikini model. Both platforms offer unique features that cater to content creators looking to engage their audience and earn income from their work. Start by visiting the official websites of OnlyFans and Fanvue, where you will find user-friendly interfaces designed to guide you through the registration process. You'll need to provide some basic information, including your email address and an appealing username that resonates with the vibrant persona of your AI influencer.

Once you've filled out the necessary information, it's time to verify your identity. This step is crucial for both platforms, as they prioritize the safety and security of their creators and subscribers. You will likely be asked to upload a valid identification document, such as a driver's license or passport. Don't fret; this process is straightforward and ensures that your account is set up correctly. After verification, you can dive into customizing your profile to reflect the unique aesthetics of your AI influencer. Choose a captivating profile picture and write a compelling bio that showcases your model's personality and the type of content subscribers can expect.

Next, you'll want to explore the monetization options available on both platforms. OnlyFans offers a subscription-based model that allows you to set a monthly fee for subscribers, while Fanvue provides flexibility with pay-per-view content and tips. Determine which model aligns best with your goals and audience. You might even consider a combination of both to maximize your earning potential. Setting competitive pricing is essential; research similar accounts to gauge what works in your niche and attract your target audience. Remember, it's about creating value that keeps subscribers coming back for more!

Creating engaging content is the heart of your success on OnlyFans and Fanvue. Plan a content calendar that includes a mix of stunning bikini shots, behind-the-scenes glimpses, and interactive posts that invite subscriber participation. Consider hosting live Q&A sessions or exclusive photo shoots that make your audience feel included in your journey. The more you engage with your subscribers, the more loyal they will become, which translates into consistent income. Use the platforms' tools to analyze your content performance and adjust your strategies to cater to your audience's preferences.

Finally, promote your OnlyFans and Fanvue accounts across your other social media channels, especially Instagram. Utilize eye-catching visuals and compelling calls-to-action to drive traffic to your profiles. Collaborating with other influencers or participating in online communities can also expand your reach. As your follower count grows, continually assess your branding and marketing strategies to ensure they align with your evolving AI influencer model. With dedication and creativity, your OnlyFans and Fanvue accounts will thrive, paving the way for a successful monetization journey!

Creating Exclusive Content for Subscribers

Creating exclusive content for subscribers is a game-changer in the world of AI influencers, especially in the bikini modeling niche. By offering unique, high-quality content, you can cultivate a loyal fan base that is eager to engage and support your AI model. The key to this exclusivity lies not only in the quality of the content but also in the creativity you bring to the table. Think beyond the typical posts and explore innovative formats that can captivate your audience.

Start by understanding your audience's preferences and interests. Conduct polls or surveys to gauge what types of content excite them the most. This could range from behind-the-scenes footage of the AI model's creation process to personalized messages tailored to individual subscribers. The more you involve your audience in the content creation process, the more valued they will feel. Utilize this feedback to craft exclusive photo sets, videos, or even live streams that showcase your AI influencer in ways that regular followers will not experience.

In addition to visual content, consider offering exclusive perks that enhance the subscriber experience. This could include access to special events, virtual meet-and-greets with your AI model, or even interactive sessions where fans can suggest themes for upcoming shoots. By creating a sense of community around your exclusive offerings, you not only foster deeper connections with your subscribers but also encourage word-of-mouth promotion. When fans feel like they are part of something special, they are more likely to share their experiences with others and attract new subscribers.

Don't forget to leverage the power of storytelling in your exclusive content. Create narratives that resonate with your audience, incorporating elements of fantasy and escapism that a bikini model can embody. Use captions and descriptions that draw subscribers into the world of your AI influencer, making them feel like they are part of an ongoing story. This narrative approach can transform simple photos or videos into engaging experiences that subscribers will eagerly anticipate.

Finally, regularly evaluate and adapt your exclusive content strategy. Keep an eye on engagement metrics and subscriber feedback to identify what works and what doesn't. This iterative process ensures that you remain aligned with your audience's evolving tastes and preferences. By continuously innovating and refining your content, you can maintain excitement and interest, ensuring your AI influencer remains a standout success in the crowded landscape of social media.

Chapter 7: Marketing Your AI Influencer

Developing a Marketing Plan

Developing a marketing plan is a crucial step in successfully launching your AI influencer bikini model on platforms like Instagram, Fanvue, or OnlyFans. To stand out in a competitive market, you need to create a strategic roadmap that outlines how you will promote your brand, engage your audience, and ultimately drive monetization. Start by clearly defining your target audience. Who are they? What are their interests and preferences? Understanding your audience will allow you to tailor your content and marketing efforts to attract and retain followers who are genuinely interested in your AI influencer.

Next, establish your unique selling proposition (USP). What makes your AI influencer bikini model different from others? This could be the model's distinctive personality, style, or even the technology behind its creation. Emphasizing these unique traits in your marketing materials will help you create a memorable brand image. Incorporate eye-catching visuals and engaging narratives that resonate with your audience. Remember, in the world of social media, visuals are everything. High-quality images, videos, and graphics will capture attention and encourage potential followers to explore your content further.

Once you have a clear understanding of your audience and a strong USP, it's time to outline your marketing strategies. Use a mix of organic and paid marketing techniques to maximize your reach. Organic strategies like collaborations with other influencers, engaging with followers through comments and direct messages, and leveraging user-generated content can build a loyal community around your AI influencer. On the other hand, paid advertising on platforms like Instagram can provide a significant boost to your visibility. Experiment with different ad formats, targeting options, and budgets to find what works best for your brand.

To keep your audience engaged, develop a content calendar that outlines your posting schedule, themes, and types of content. Consistency is key in maintaining interest and building anticipation among your followers. Incorporate various content formats, such as behind-the-scenes footage, styling tips, or interactive polls, to create a dynamic feed that keeps your audience coming back for more. Don't forget to monitor engagement metrics to assess which types of content resonate most with your audience, allowing you to refine your approach over time.

Finally, consider how you will monetize your AI influencer bikini model. Explore different revenue streams, such as sponsored posts, merchandise sales, or subscription-based content on platforms like Fanvue or OnlyFans. Craft compelling calls to action that encourage followers to support your brand, whether through purchasing exclusive content or joining membership programs. By developing a comprehensive marketing plan that encompasses audience understanding, unique branding, strategic engagement, and monetization, you'll be well on your way to turning your AI influencer bikini model into a thriving online sensation.

Leveraging Social Media Advertising

Leveraging social media advertising is a game-changer for anyone looking to create and monetize an AI influencer bikini model. The landscape of digital marketing has evolved dramatically, and platforms like Instagram, Fanvue, and OnlyFans provide a fertile ground for innovative advertising strategies. By harnessing the power of social media advertising, creators can elevate their AI models, reach wider audiences, and significantly boost revenue. The key is to understand how to effectively utilize these platforms to your advantage.

First, identify your target audience and craft ads that resonate with them. The bikini niche is vibrant and diverse, attracting a wide range of followers. Tailor your advertising campaigns to appeal to specific demographics, be it fitness enthusiasts, beach lovers, or fashion-forward individuals. Utilize tools such as Instagram Insights to analyze user behavior and preferences, ensuring your ads are not only eye-catching but also strategically aligned with what your audience desires. Personalized content is more likely to convert viewers into loyal subscribers or customers.

Next, leverage the unique features of each platform. Instagram's visually driven content is perfect for showcasing stunning imagery of your AI influencer. Use eye-catching visuals combined with strong calls to action to engage users. Meanwhile, Fanvue and OnlyFans offer different avenues for interaction, such as exclusive content or behind-the-scenes looks. Promoting these unique selling points through targeted ads can entice followers to subscribe or engage more deeply with your content. Experiment with ad formats, from stories to reels, to discover what captivates your audience the most.

Collaboration is another powerful strategy in social media advertising. Partnering with other influencers or brands can amplify your reach exponentially. Consider collaborating with established bikini brands or fellow influencers in related niches to cross-promote each other's content. This not only enhances credibility but also exposes your AI influencer to a broader audience. Joint giveaways, shout-outs, or co-created content can generate buzz and drive traffic to your profiles, creating a win-win situation for all parties involved.

Lastly, track and analyze your advertising efforts meticulously. Use analytics tools to monitor the performance of your ads across platforms. Understanding which ads convert and which do not allows for continuous improvement and optimization of your campaigns. Adjust your strategies based on data insights, testing different approaches to find the most effective methods for engaging your audience. By consistently refining your advertising tactics, you can ensure that your AI influencer bikini model not only gains followers but also maximizes monetization potential across Instagram, Fanvue, and OnlyFans.

Engaging in Influencer Partnerships

Engaging in influencer partnerships is a thrilling opportunity to elevate your AI influencer bikini model's visibility and monetization potential. By collaborating with established personalities in the fashion, beauty, and lifestyle sectors, you can tap into their audience and enhance your model's credibility. The key is to choose influencers whose brand aligns closely with your model's aesthetics and values. This synergy not only strengthens your marketing efforts but also fosters a genuine connection with audiences who appreciate both your model and the influencers they follow.

When seeking out influencer partnerships, consider the reach and engagement rates of potential collaborators. A micro-influencer, for instance, may have a smaller following but often enjoys higher engagement levels. These influencers are highly relatable and can create authentic content that resonates with their audience. Crafting a compelling pitch that highlights mutual benefits, such as co-branded content, giveaways, or exclusive collaborations, will encourage influencers to join forces with your AI model. This collaborative spirit can generate buzz and excitement, drawing new followers to your platforms.

The content you create with influencers should be visually striking and aligned with current trends in the bikini and swimwear niche. Think vibrant beach scenes, playful poses, and interactive stories that invite followers to engage. Use this opportunity to showcase your AI model in unique ways that highlight its capabilities, whether through innovative fashion choices or stunning visual effects. Captivating content not only makes for great social media posts but creates shareable moments that can spread like wildfire across platforms, introducing your model to new audiences.

Don't forget to leverage the power of analytics to measure the success of your influencer partnerships. Track engagement metrics, follower growth, and conversion rates to understand what resonates best with your audience. This data-driven approach will allow you to refine future collaborations and optimize content strategies. Celebrate the wins, learn from the challenges, and use insights gathered to fuel the next wave of influencer partnerships, ensuring your AI influencer bikini model continues to thrive in a competitive landscape.

As you embark on this exciting journey of influencer partnerships, remember that authenticity is key. Maintain a genuine voice and stay true to your model's identity, even while collaborating with others. This authenticity will shine through in your content, fostering trust and loyalty among followers. Embrace the creativity and excitement that comes with building these partnerships, and watch as your AI influencer bikini model becomes a sought-after name in the industry, paving the way for greater monetization opportunities on platforms like Instagram, Fanvue, and OnlyFans.

Chapter 8: Navigating Challenges and Ethical Considerations

Addressing Potential Criticism

In the rapidly evolving landscape of digital content creation, the emergence of AI influencers, particularly in niches like bikini modeling, invites a host of potential criticisms. It's essential to address these concerns head-on, not just to fortify your position but to inspire confidence in your audience. The conversation often centers around authenticity and the potential for AI-generated content to overshadow human creators. However, by redefining what authenticity means in the digital age, we can celebrate the innovative possibilities that AI influencers bring to the table.

One of the most common criticisms revolves around the idea that AI influencers lack the genuine human touch. Detractors argue that traditional influencers offer relatability and emotional connection that an AI model simply cannot provide. Yet, this perspective overlooks the unique engagement strategies that AI influencers can utilize. By analyzing audience preferences and tailoring content to resonate with followers, AI models can foster a different but equally engaging form of connection. This adaptability can lead to a more personalized experience for fans, showcasing the potential for AI to enhance rather than detract from the influencer experience.

Another point of contention is the ethical implications of using AI in modeling, especially within the bikini niche. Critics may voice concerns about objectification, body image issues, and the unrealistic standards that AI-generated content might perpetuate. Addressing this criticism involves a commitment to inclusivity and diversity in representation. By programming AI influencers to embody a range of body types and styles, you can challenge conventional beauty norms and promote a healthier dialogue around body positivity. This proactive approach not only mitigates criticism but also positions your brand as a pioneer in advocating for a more inclusive digital space.

Concerns about the monetization aspect also arise, particularly regarding the potential for AI influencers to overshadow human creators. While it's true that AI influencers can streamline content production and reduce costs, they can also create new opportunities for collaboration and innovation. Imagine partnering with human influencers where AI models complement their styles and enhance their reach. This synergy can open up new avenues for creativity, allowing both AI and human influencers to thrive in a mutually beneficial ecosystem. Emphasizing collaboration over competition is key to addressing this criticism effectively.

Finally, fostering transparency regarding the use of AI in influencer marketing is crucial. Many consumers today are becoming increasingly savvy and discerning about the content they consume. By openly communicating the AI's role in content creation, you can build trust and credibility with your audience. This transparency not only addresses potential skepticism but also invites followers to engage in a dialogue about the future of digital influencers. By embracing the conversation around AI and its implications, you position yourself as a thought leader in this exciting new frontier, paving the way for a successful and sustainable brand.

Understanding Copyright and AI Ownership

Understanding copyright in the context of AI ownership is crucial for anyone looking to create and monetize an AI influencer, particularly in the vibrant world of bikini modeling on platforms like Instagram, Fanvue, or OnlyFans. As you embark on this exciting journey, it's essential to grasp the legal landscape surrounding the content your AI generates. Copyright laws are designed to protect original works of authorship, which raises the question: who owns the rights to content created by an AI? This understanding will empower you to navigate potential legal pitfalls and maximize your profit potential.

When we discuss AI-generated content, we enter a gray area of copyright law. Typically, copyright protection is granted to works created by human authors. However, as technology advances, the lines become increasingly blurred. For AI influencers, the content generated—from photos and videos to captions and posts—poses unique challenges. Engaging with legal experts who specialize in intellectual property can provide clarity and help ensure that your AI influencer operates within the bounds of the law while maximizing creative output.

Moreover, the ownership of AI-generated content is often tied to the specific algorithms and data sets used to train the AI. If you've developed your own AI model, you likely hold copyright over the output it generates. However, if you are utilizing existing AI tools or platforms, the terms of service may dictate the ownership rights. This is where due diligence becomes vital. Carefully reviewing agreements can help you secure your rights and avoid any potential disputes that could jeopardize your influencer's brand.

In the lively world of social media, the appeal of unique and engaging content is paramount. Therefore, understanding how copyright relates to your AI influencer allows you to create distinctive, original posts that resonate with your audience. Leveraging the unique capabilities of AI can lead to innovative content creation, whether it's personalized interactions or stunning visual presentations. By establishing a robust copyright strategy from the outset, you can focus on creating captivating experiences for your followers while safeguarding your intellectual property.

Ultimately, understanding copyright and AI ownership is not just about compliance; it's about empowerment. With the right knowledge, you can confidently navigate this dynamic landscape, ensuring that your AI influencer thrives in the competitive realms of Instagram, Fanvue, and OnlyFans. Embrace this opportunity to innovate and captivate, knowing that you have a solid grasp of the legal aspects that underpin your creative endeavors. This knowledge will not only protect your work but also fuel your passion for building a successful and monetizable AI influencer brand.

Maintaining Authenticity in an AI-Driven World

In an era where technology advances at lightning speed, maintaining authenticity in an AI-driven world is both a challenge and an opportunity for aspiring influencers. As you embark on the journey of creating and monetizing an AI influencer bikini model, it's crucial to remember that authenticity remains the cornerstone of successful engagement. Your audience craves genuine connections, and even though your model is AI-generated, the persona you craft must resonate with real emotions and experiences. This authenticity will set your brand apart in a saturated market.

To cultivate authenticity, embrace storytelling as a powerful tool. Share the journey of your AI model, from concept to creation. Highlight the unique attributes that make your model relatable and appealing. Craft narratives around her adventures, aspirations, and lifestyle that mirror those of your target audience. By weaving in relatable stories, you'll foster a deeper connection with followers, making them feel like they're part of your influencer's journey. This connection is essential for building loyalty and encouraging engagement across platforms like Instagram, Fanvue, or OnlyFans.

Engagement doesn't stop at storytelling; it also involves interaction. Actively responding to comments, messages, and feedback creates a dialogue between your AI influencer and her audience. Utilize polls, Q&A sessions, and live streams to invite your followers into the conversation. This humanizes your AI model, making her seem less like a digital creation and more like a friend who values her community. Authentic engagement fosters trust, which is essential for monetizing your influencer effectively.

In addition to engagement, transparency is vital in maintaining authenticity. Be open about the AI nature of your model while emphasizing the creativity and innovation behind her persona. Educate your audience about the technology that powers your influencer, demystifying artificial intelligence. This transparency not only builds trust but also showcases your commitment to authenticity. When followers understand the effort and technology behind the model, they may feel even more connected to her, enhancing their loyalty and willingness to support her endeavors.

Finally, remember that authenticity doesn't mean perfection. Embrace the quirks and imperfections that come with being an AI influencer. Incorporate humor, spontaneity, and even moments of vulnerability into your content. This approach will resonate with your audience, humanizing your model and making her more relatable. In a world where everyone is vying for attention, being real and approachable will allow your AI influencer bikini model to shine and thrive, creating a vibrant community that's eager to engage and invest in her journey.

Chapter 9: Scaling Your Empire

Expanding Your Brand Beyond Bikinis

Expanding your brand beyond bikinis is an exhilarating venture that opens up a world of possibilities for your AI influencer model. While your primary focus may start with swimwear, there's an entire universe of opportunities waiting to be explored. From fashion collaborations to lifestyle content, the potential to diversify your offerings is not only exciting but essential for long-term growth. Embracing variety will keep your audience engaged and enhance your overall brand appeal. The journey of expansion not only elevates your influencer status but can also significantly increase your income streams.

One of the most effective ways to broaden your brand is by venturing into athleisure wear. The fitness and wellness industry has seen explosive growth, and by integrating activewear into your AI model's content, you can tap into a thriving market. Showcase your model engaging in various fitness activities while sporting stylish workout gear. This not only emphasizes a healthy lifestyle but also attracts partnerships with athletic brands eager to promote their products through your influencer's platform. By aligning with the wellness trend, you'll resonate with a broader audience while maintaining your core identity in the fashion realm.

Another exciting avenue to explore is lifestyle and home decor. Curate content that reflects your AI model's personality beyond swimwear, such as interior design tips, travel adventures, or even cooking recipes. This approach allows followers to connect with your brand on a deeper level, fostering loyalty and engagement. Collaborate with brands that align with these lifestyle themes and introduce your audience to a wider array of products and services. This cross-pollination can lead to lucrative partnerships and sponsorships that further enhance your brand's visibility and profitability.

Additionally, consider delving into digital products and exclusive content offerings. Create e-books, courses, or subscription-based content that provides value to your audience. Topics could range from style guides to fitness routines, all while maintaining the signature flair of your AI influencer. By offering these digital products, you not only diversify your revenue streams but also establish your brand as an authority in multiple niches. Fans will appreciate the extra value and are likely to become more invested in your brand, increasing their likelihood of supporting your monetization efforts on platforms like OnlyFans or Fanvue.

Finally, don't underestimate the power of community engagement. Building a dedicated fan base can be the backbone of expanding your brand. Utilize social media platforms to host live Q&A sessions, polls, and interactive content that encourages followers to share their thoughts and preferences. This not only fosters a sense of belonging but also provides valuable insights into what your audience craves. Engaging with your community will spark new ideas for content and collaborations, allowing you to creatively expand your brand beyond bikinis while ensuring your model remains relatable and relevant in an ever-evolving digital landscape.

Exploring New Platforms and Opportunities

Exploring new platforms and opportunities is essential for anyone looking to elevate their AI influencer bikini model to new heights. As the landscape of social media and content creation continues to evolve, staying ahead of the curve means not only understanding existing platforms like Instagram, Fanvue, and OnlyFans but also being open to emerging opportunities that can amplify your reach and revenue. By tapping into the latest trends and technologies, you can ensure your AI influencer stands out in an increasingly crowded space.

One of the most exciting aspects of exploring new platforms is the potential for unique audience engagement. Each platform has its own set of features and demographics, allowing you to tailor your content to resonate with specific audiences. For instance, TikTok's short-form video format is perfect for showcasing your AI bikini model's personality through fun, engaging clips. Meanwhile, platforms like Patreon offer a subscription-based model, where fans can access exclusive content and behind-the-scenes looks at your creative process. Embracing these diverse platforms can lead to new revenue streams and a more dedicated fanbase.

Moreover, the rise of virtual reality (VR) and augmented reality (AR) presents thrilling opportunities for AI influencers. Imagine creating immersive experiences where followers can interact with your AI model in a virtual beach setting or try on different bikini styles through AR filters. This level of engagement not only captivates your audience but also encourages them to share their experiences with others, effectively expanding your reach. By experimenting with these cutting-edge technologies, you can position your AI influencer as a pioneer in the industry, attracting attention and investment.

Collaboration is another vital aspect of exploring new opportunities. Partnering with other creators or brands can open doors to new audiences and innovative content ideas. For example, collaborating with fashion brands for exclusive bikini launches can create buzz and drive sales, while working with fellow influencers can result in cross-promotion that benefits all parties involved. By actively seeking out partnerships and networking within your niche, you can establish a powerful presence that resonates across multiple platforms.

Finally, don't underestimate the power of analytics and feedback in your exploration of new opportunities. Monitoring performance metrics across different platforms will help you understand what resonates with your audience and where adjustments are needed. Utilize tools that provide insights into engagement, demographics, and content performance to make informed decisions about your strategy. By being proactive and responsive to your audience's preferences, you can continuously refine your approach, ensuring that your AI influencer bikini model remains relevant and profitable in a fast-paced digital environment.

Building a Team to Support Your Vision

Building a team to support your vision is crucial in the fast-paced world of AI influencers. As you embark on the journey to create and monetize your AI influencer bikini model, assembling a talented and dedicated team can make all the difference. This team should consist of individuals who share your passion and are excited about pushing the boundaries of creativity and technology. By surrounding yourself with like-minded professionals, you'll cultivate an environment that fosters innovation, ensuring that your AI influencer stands out in a crowded market.

Start by identifying key roles that will be essential to your project. A skilled AI developer is at the heart of your endeavor, responsible for creating the digital persona that embodies your vision. Pair this expertise with a dynamic social media strategist who understands the nuances of platforms like Instagram, Fanvue, and OnlyFans. They will help craft your influencer's online presence, ensuring that every post resonates with your target audience. Additionally, consider hiring a marketing specialist who can devise effective strategies to monetize your influencer, turning views and likes into tangible revenue streams.

Collaboration is key in this creative process. Regular brainstorming sessions can ignite innovative ideas and strategies that elevate your influencer's appeal. Encourage your team to share their unique perspectives, as diversity in thought often leads to groundbreaking concepts. Emphasize the importance of open communication, so everyone feels empowered to contribute. When each team member understands their role and how it fits into the larger vision, you harness collective energy that propels your project forward.

As you build your team, prioritize hiring individuals who are not only skilled but also share your enthusiasm for the project. A team that believes in the potential of your AI influencer will work harder and be more invested in its success. Look for those who demonstrate creativity, adaptability, and a passion for technology. Their excitement will be infectious, inspiring everyone involved to give their best and align their efforts with your vision.

Lastly, don't forget to celebrate your achievements, no matter how small. Recognizing milestones and successes fosters a positive team culture and keeps morale high. This energy translates into better collaboration and innovation as your team continues to develop your AI influencer. With a strong, passionate team by your side, you are well on your way to creating a captivating AI bikini model that not only engages audiences but also paves the way for successful monetization on various platforms.

Chapter 10: The Future of AI Influencers

Emerging Trends in AI Technology

Emerging trends in AI technology are reshaping the landscape for influencers, especially in niche markets like bikini modeling. As advancements in machine learning and computer vision continue to evolve, the potential for creating hyper-realistic AI models is becoming a reality. Imagine a virtual influencer that not only embodies the latest fashion trends but also interacts with followers in real-time, adapting its persona based on audience preferences. This dynamic capability opens new avenues for engagement, allowing brands to leverage AI influencers in ways that traditional models simply cannot match.

One of the most exciting trends is the rise of generative adversarial networks (GANs), which are enabling the creation of lifelike images and videos of AI influencers. These tools allow for the customization of features, outfits, and poses, ensuring that the AI model aligns perfectly with branding objectives. As a creator in the bikini modeling niche, this means you can offer a unique, tailor-made experience to your audience. Picture an AI model that can showcase a variety of swimwear styles, colors, and settings, appealing to diverse tastes and preferences, all while maintaining an authentic connection with followers.

Another noteworthy trend is the integration of AI-driven analytics tools that provide insights into audience behaviors and preferences. These tools can analyze engagement metrics and social media trends, helping you refine your content strategy. By understanding what resonates with your audience, you can curate posts that drive higher interaction rates and increase monetization opportunities. This data-driven approach empowers you to make informed decisions that enhance your AI influencer's visibility and appeal, ultimately leading to greater success on platforms like Instagram, Fanvue, or OnlyFans.

Furthermore, the incorporation of augmented reality (AR) technology is revolutionizing how followers interact with AI influencers. With AR filters and effects, users can experience immersive content that allows them to virtually 'try on' swimwear or accessories showcased by the AI model. This interactive element not only boosts engagement but also encourages followers to share their experiences on social media, effectively amplifying your reach. As a creator, embracing AR technology can set your AI influencer apart from the competition, creating buzz and excitement that drives followers to your platforms.

Lastly, the ethical considerations surrounding AI influencers are coming into sharper focus. As creators, it's crucial to navigate these discussions thoughtfully, ensuring transparency and authenticity. Building trust with your audience will be vital in maintaining long-term relationships, especially in a space that is still relatively new. By addressing ethical concerns head-on and promoting responsible AI usage, you can position your AI bikini model as a leader in the market, attracting collaborations with brands that value integrity and innovation. Embracing these emerging trends will not only enhance your brand but also pave the way for a successful and sustainable future in the evolving world of AI influencers.

Predictions for the Influencer Market

The influencer market is on the brink of a stunning transformation, driven by advancements in artificial intelligence and the growing demand for unique digital personas. As we step into a new era, AI influencers are set to captivate audiences in ways that traditional influencers cannot. The ability to create hyper-realistic models who embody ideal beauty standards while appealing to diverse audiences represents a golden opportunity for brands and creators alike. Expect to see AI bikini models breaking the mold, becoming trendsetters, and redefining beauty standards, all while engaging millions of followers across platforms like Instagram, Fanvue, and OnlyFans.

With the rise of AI technology, we can predict a surge in the personalization of content. Viewers crave authenticity, and AI influencers can deliver tailored experiences that resonate deeply with their followers. Imagine an AI bikini model that learns from audience interactions, adapting her style, tone, and messaging based on real-time feedback. This level of customization will not only enhance user engagement but will also empower brands to connect with their target audience more effectively. As influencers become more attuned to their followers' preferences, we will witness an era of unprecedented interaction that will redefine influencer marketing.

The monetization strategies available to AI influencers will also evolve dramatically. Gone are the days when brands relied solely on sponsored posts. The future will see AI bikini models leveraging advanced data analytics to create personalized affiliate marketing campaigns, subscription-based content, and exclusive merchandise. Platforms like Fanvue and OnlyFans will become essential for monetizing niche audiences, providing creators with tools to maximize revenue streams. As these models gain traction, we can expect an influx of innovative business models that challenge traditional influencer marketing norms.

Furthermore, the growing acceptance of virtual influencers will lead to new collaborations between AI models and human influencers. This fusion will create dynamic content that blends the best of both worlds. Imagine a well-known human influencer partnering with an AI bikini model for a campaign, combining their unique strengths to appeal to a broader audience. These partnerships will not only enhance the creative landscape but will also introduce exciting opportunities for cross-promotion, expanding reach and engagement across various platforms.

Lastly, as the influencer market evolves, ethical considerations around AI models will become increasingly significant. Audiences will demand transparency and authenticity, pushing creators to establish trust with their followers. This will lead to a new wave of responsible AI usage, where influencers prioritize the well-being of their communities. By addressing issues such as representation, consent, and digital identity, the influencer market will cultivate a healthier environment that respects both creators and followers. The future is bright, and the potential for AI influencers in the bikini model niche is limitless, promising an exhilarating journey for those ready to embrace this transformation.

Staying Ahead of the Curve

Staying ahead of the curve in the dynamic world of AI influencer bikini modeling is crucial for anyone looking to thrive on platforms like Instagram, Fanvue, or OnlyFans. As technology evolves, so do the trends and preferences of audiences. To ensure your AI influencer remains relevant and captivating, it's essential to keep a pulse on emerging developments in artificial intelligence, social media algorithms, and audience engagement strategies. Embracing these changes allows you to create content that resonates with your followers while setting you apart from the competition.

One of the most effective ways to stay ahead is by continuously experimenting with new AI technologies. For instance, utilizing advanced generative models can enhance the realism and appeal of your AI influencer's images and videos. Staying updated on tools that improve facial recognition, voice synthesis, and even motion capture can elevate your content, making it more lifelike and engaging. By integrating the latest advancements, you not only boost the aesthetic quality of your posts but also solidify your position as a trendsetter in the niche.

Engagement with your audience is another key factor in maintaining your influencer's popularity. Regularly analyzing feedback, comments, and social media trends will provide valuable insights into what your followers crave. Use this information to adapt your content strategy and introduce interactive elements like polls, Q&As, or behind-the-scenes glimpses of the AI modeling process. By fostering a sense of community and involvement, you create loyal followers who feel personally connected to your brand, amplifying your influencer's reach.

Networking with other creators and industry experts can also provide fresh perspectives and innovative ideas. Participate in online forums, attend virtual conferences, or collaborate with fellow influencers to exchange knowledge and strategies. These connections can lead to exciting collaborations that enhance your AI influencer's visibility and introduce you to new audiences. Remember, the influencer landscape is constantly evolving, and building a robust network can open doors to opportunities that keep you at the forefront of the industry.

Lastly, don't underestimate the power of ongoing education. Regularly investing time in learning about digital marketing trends, social media strategies, and the latest developments in AI technology will empower you to make informed decisions. Online courses, webinars, and industry reports are invaluable resources that can keep your skills sharp and your strategies effective. By committing to continuous learning, you'll not only stay ahead of the curve but also inspire confidence in your audience about your expertise in creating and monetizing an AI influencer bikini model.

www.ingramcontent.com/pod-product-compliance
Lightning Source LLC
LaVergne TN
LVHW051622050326
832903LV00033B/4616